Decodabl

MW00657196

A Little Mat

Written by Alex Altman
Illustrated by Mary Stern

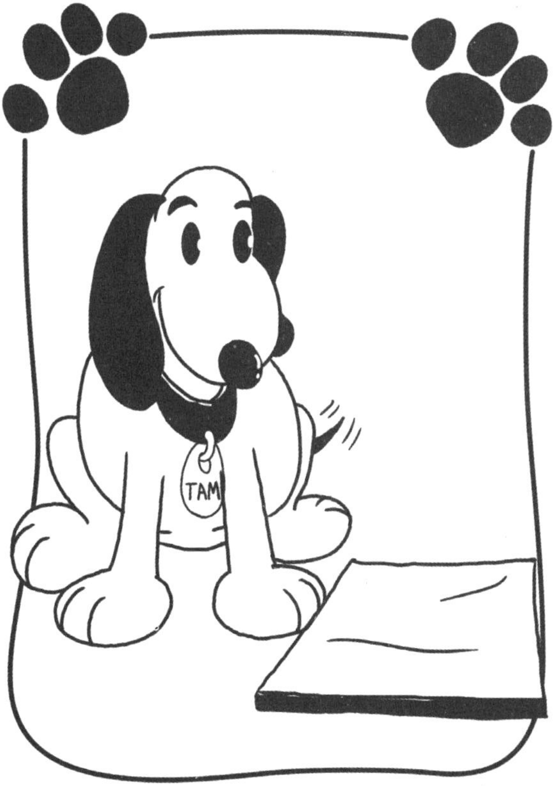

Phonics Skill

Short a

am Tam mat at

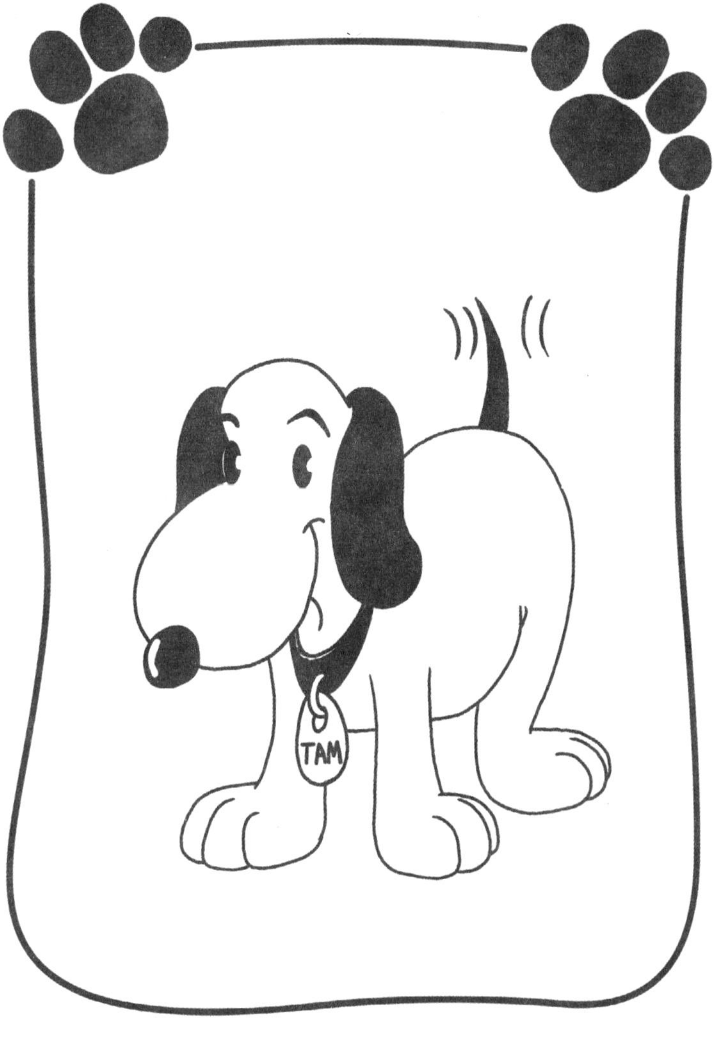

I am Tam.

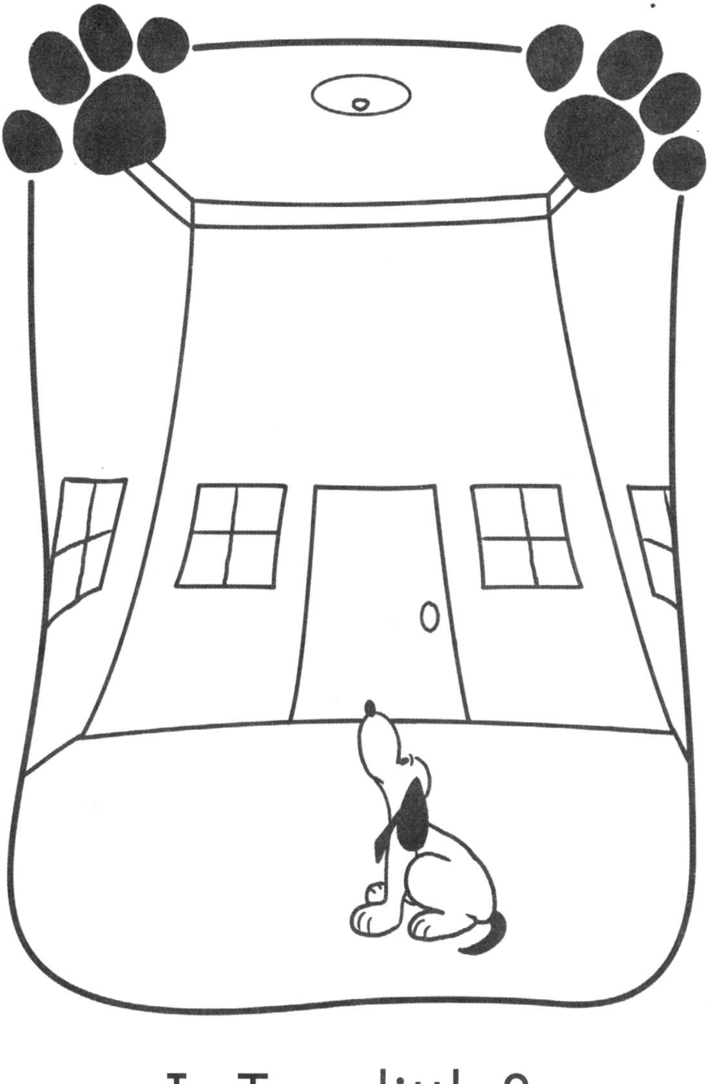

Is Tam little?

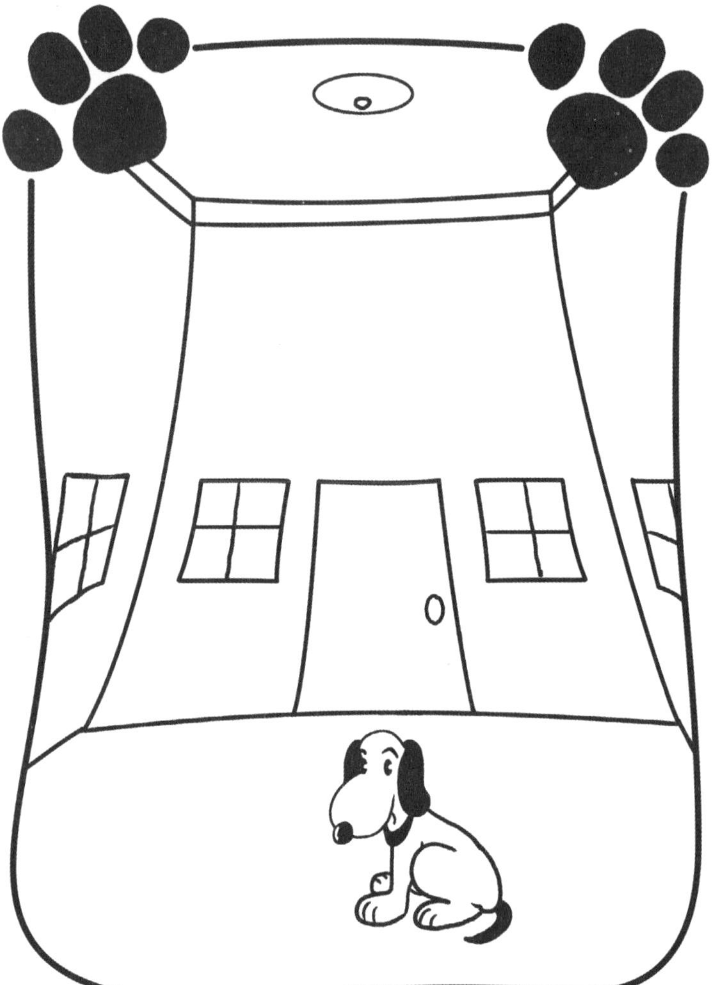

Tam is little.

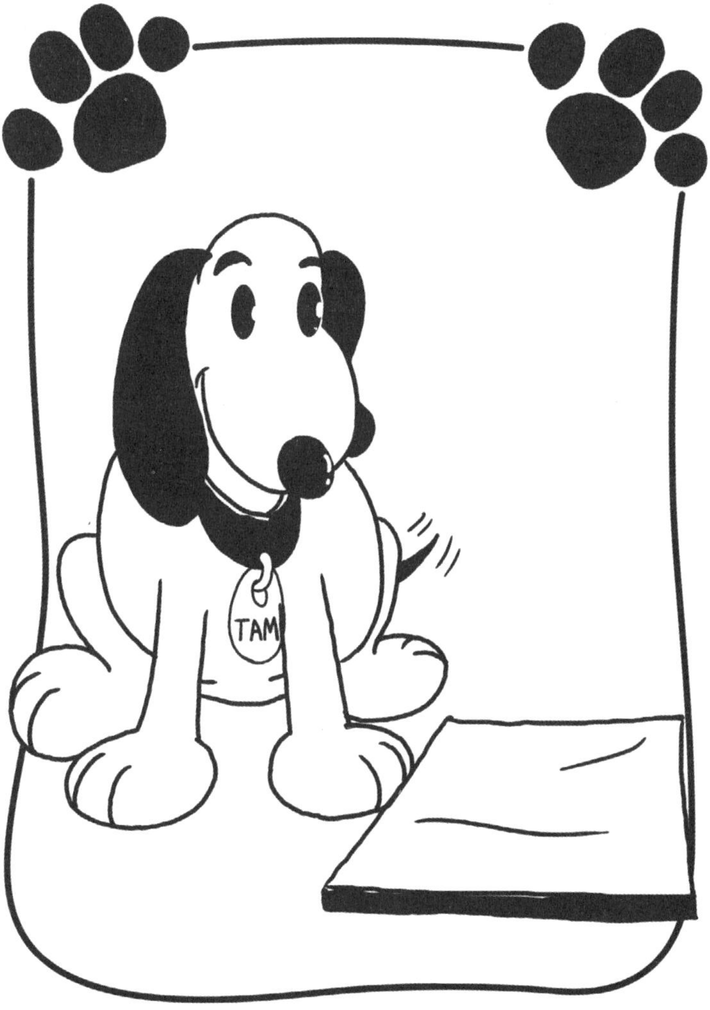

I have a mat.

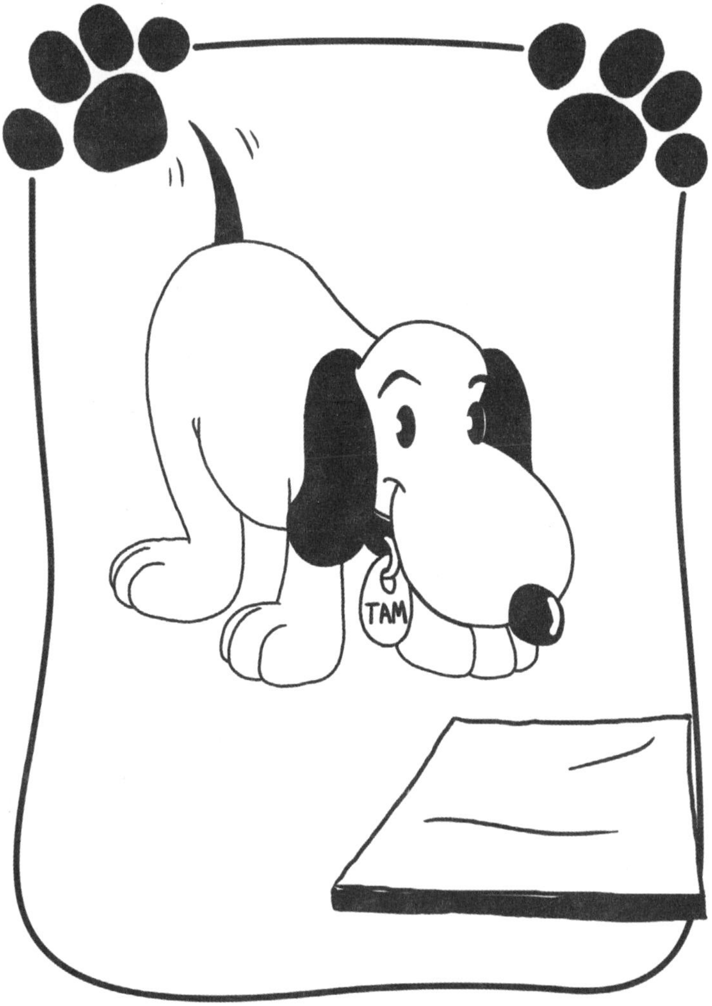

Is the mat little?

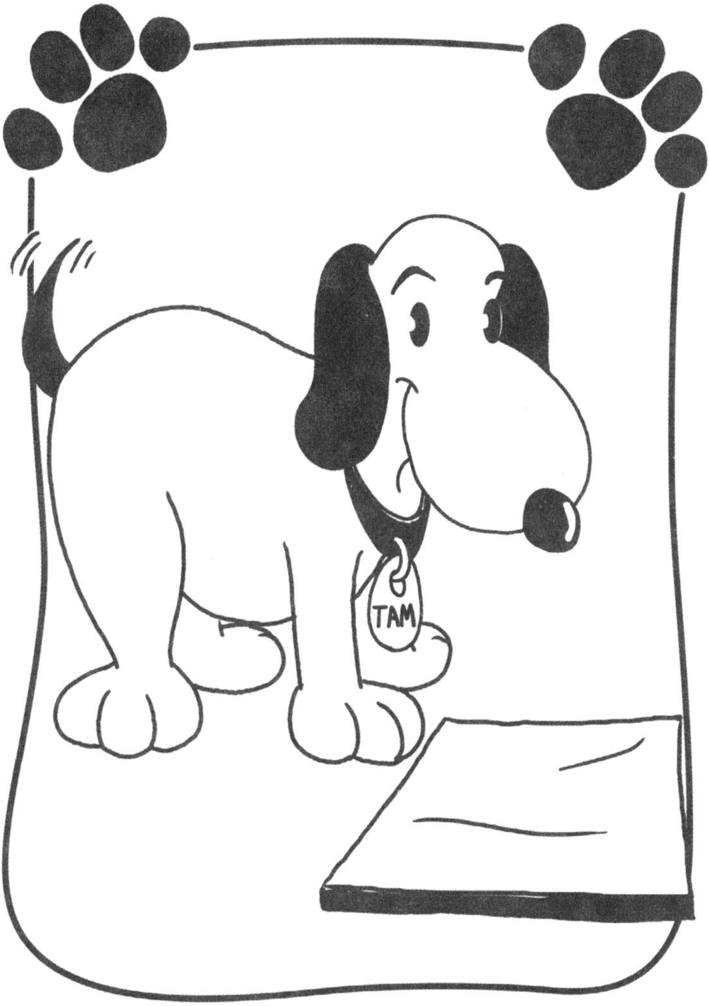

The mat is little.

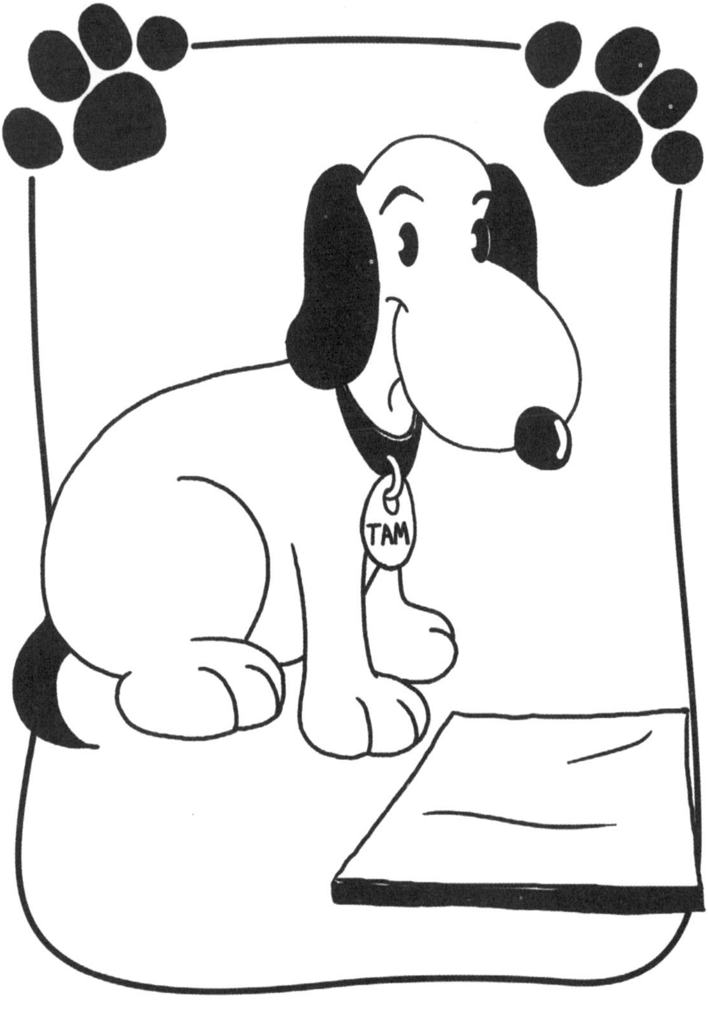

Tam is at the mat.